The Wind amongst the Ruins

A Childhood in Macao

Edith Jorge De Martini

VANTAGE PRESS
New York

For those who in the past stood against the wind to hold standing the ruins so that we and the generations to come will remember.

For all the natives of my island for whom the wind was stronger and who are scattered around the world but still remember and feel nostalgic . . .

For my daughters, who are the future.

For Katiana.

Contents

Foreword

Buenos Aires, Argentina, February 1986

Strange that I felt this sudden urge to write. Strange and frightening! Word after word, scene after scene, recollections so vivid that it seems I am travelling backwards forty-five years through a time tunnel towards my childhood, towards my birthplace.

I feel this terrible pull and urge to put down on paper all that is coming into my mind, like waves from an angry sea, lashing my brain with memories longtime buried and forgotten. There is no peace! Awake, asleep, at work, at all times these scenes from my past come forward, wanting to be transformed into words, and I write, I write! Day after day I race against time, trying to keep up with the floods of memories. I can even see the shape of the whole book I am supposed to write, I can even see the ending but my hands are slower in putting down on paper all that my mind dictates.

The words are pictures as vivid as if they were scenes of only yesterday, and pictures are words so rich that I wonder where I find them. It is frightening, and I can't explain to myself what is happening inside my soul. Why all this? I have never thought of writing a book! I am a painter; brushes and paints are my tools. But words? Where did they come from and why these special years of my past? Why are they so vivid, so easy to remember; why? . . .

Then suddenly, a few weeks after it all started, all was silent. The urge, the pull, the flow of words were gone. I put away my typewriter and told my husband I was stopping. I am at peace finally. I no longer feel possessed by my memories, but the book is not finished! My hands were not fast enough, although in my mind

I have registered everything up to the end. My husband tried to encourage me to go on, but there were no more waves, no more ghosts from the past talking to me. If I ever finish this book I will really have to depend on how much I will be able to dig from my memory, how well I can manage to find my way back to my inspiration; I will have to search my soul to find the words myself, words floating in this sudden silence.

A few days later I learnt that my maternal grandmother, who shares so many pages of this book with me, died on the same day I stopped writing. She had been bedridden for two years, a vegetable, unable to communicate with anybody. She who is such an important part of my recollections and my growing-up years, was she the ghostwriter? Did she want me to remember, to go backwards, to travel with her through her mind? Was she leaving me the best legacy she owned: her past, my beginnings?

I want to believe so, and for her sake I shall continue where she left me. I shall try to find her words and make her live through my pages, my book, so that she becomes the "wind blowing amongst the ruins," waking them up to stir all our memories.

She died alone, so far from her roots, from that fascinating island where she was born, lived, and built her family. And I am still farther away in a country where there is no knowledge of that exotic place where I belonged, so that maybe, in her last moments, she held out her hand and took the small child that exists in me, and we both crossed this great length of time separating the present from the past and she made me learn to reach out for my roots, to know myself better.

Author's Note

Macao is located on the southeastern coast of China, some forty miles west-southwest of the British colony of Hong Kong at the mouth of the Pearl River. Together with the islands of Taipa and Coloane, it consists only of a total of 15.5 square kilometers (6 square miles). At present, Macao has over 400,000 inhabitants, 98 percent of whom are Chinese.

Macao is the oldest European settlement in the East. The first Portuguese navigator to sail along the South China coast, Jorge Alvares, reached the area in 1513. But only in 1554 were the Portuguese authorized to trade at the ports of Guangdong province in South China, including Macao or Hei Keang as it was known at that time. When in 1557 the Portuguese fleet helped the Chinese to defeat the pirates along those southern coasts, the emperor granted the right to the Portuguese to establish in Macao a permanent settlement. Macao became not only an important centre for trade between China, Japan, and Europe, but it was also the base for the introduction of Christianity to these remote countries. Because of its prosperity and strategic situation, many European countries were eager to seize it from Portugal, and the Dutch, in particular, tried unsuccessfully to invade the city many times.

For over four hundred years Macao has been a place where the Portuguese set down roots, raised their families, and planted their culture and religion. In the seventeenth century, when Portugal was taken over by the Spanish during the reign of the Philips, Macao defiantly never lowered the Portuguese flag and flew it proudly over the territory. When, after sixty years, the Portuguese rule was reestablished and King John IV regained his throne, in recognition of the unfailing loyalty of that territory, he granted the city the title of "City of the Name of God, Macao; There Is None More Loyal."

The Portuguese and the Chinese have, through these four centuries, shared a very pleasant and cordial relationship, which shows in many facets of the city: the mixed cultural heritage, the architectural aspects of the town, and its people, who are called the Macanese. Through so many centuries of living side by side, little by little the Chinese strain was added to the Portuguese blood and the distinct Eurasian look marked the features of the people of Macao, making them an interesting mixture of strong European looks with the softness of the Asian beauty.

In the physical aspect of the city, the grandiose colonial architectural structures have been, through the years, mostly erased by the demands of the growing population, giving way, at present, to modern high-rise buildings. But fortunately, some of the vestiges of the past have been preserved and restored to their initial beauty, to remind us of the era when Macao was a sort of Mediterranean paradise in Asia.

In 1999 the last page of this long history of Portuguese presence will be closed when Macao is returned to China. It will be a political change, a material matter only. The spiritual presence of those who lived and died in this enchanted place will linger there forever, and for the curious visitor who will walk along the cobblestone streets, the soft murmuring of the wind amongst the ruins of the old monuments will whisper once, twice, and a thousand times the story I am about to tell in this book.

Preface

Many readers going through the pages of this book will be surprised to see that I call Macao an island when in reality it is a peninsula, attached to China by a narrow strip of land. But since my early years I have always heard it called this way, and as this book deals with my past, I cannot, while writing it, disassociate myself from this idea. The following passages from the book *Seventeenth Century Macau*, by C. R. Boxer (Hong Kong: Heinemann, 1986), will perhaps explain why, in the past and during my childhood, most people thought of Macao as an island.

> The city of Maccaou or Maccauw is situated on one of the small islands along the coast of the exceedingly rich Empire of China, in 20½ degrees northern Latitude. Albeit this is called an island, yet it is so near the mainland that one can walk across dryshod on a small connecting tongue of land. In the middle of this narrow strip of and between the island and the Chinese coast is a stone wall with a gate on it.[1]

Also from the same book comes the following:

> Macao standeth at one end of a greatt Iland built on rising hills, some gardeins and trees among their houses making a pretty prospecte somwhatt resembling Goa, allthough not soe bigge; Their houses

1. A description of the city of Macao written by Marco D'Avalo and translated by C. R. Boxer, chapter 3, p. 72.

doubled tyled, and thatt plaistred over agained, for prevention of Hurracanes or violent wyndes that happen some Yeares, called by the Chinois Tuffaones, which is allso the reason (as they say) they build no high towers Nor steeples to their Churches.[2]

While writing my book, I have many times resisted the temptation of going into deeper research through history books or family memories because I want to keep this exchange of feelings and recollections between the voice of my childhood and myself now as pure, simple, and spontaneous as possible. I do not pretend to be too precise or too accurate about certain details or memories. I will just go along leisurely, led by the hand of this little girl who has opened the door of my past to me. This is our book, our own way of putting down on paper for posterity a family relationship, an experience in growing up in a place that was so unique in the past, but which now, unfortunately, with advancing progress and the exodus of its children to other shores, is losing its true noble identity.

Every time the wind blows strong over the ruins, small pieces of our history are sent tumbling down, weakening those monuments of the past. So is the way with those who have roots reaching so far back in this island; the winds of fortune, of adventure, of desire for wider horizons blow the young Macanese away from these grounds and spread them all over the world, taking along with them small pieces of our traditions, of the soul of this island; relics that gathered together could complete the puzzle of what, in reality, the nearly five centuries of the existence of Macao means in the history of our civilisation and the world.

I feel that with every departure and separation my island fades a little, becomes more remote, and burrows deeper all its treasures. Those who in the future will come to visit these exotic and historical shores will find very little of the days gone by, of the poetry that

2. A description of Macao written by Peter Mundy in 1637, chapter 2, p. 42.

hung in the air, of the elegance and pride of its colonial residences and its inhabitants, of the special people who walked its streets.

There is no way of returning to the past. But to avoid the tragic death of such an era, we have to keep it alive in our souls and in our memories so that we may pass it on to our next generation.

This is the purpose of this book. It is not a history book, nor is it a work of fiction. It is simply a book of memories with no other value than to demonstrate the deep love both the little girl and this grown woman share for our roots.

Acknowledgments

My grateful thanks to family and friends who, throughout my first experience in the literary world, gave support and assistance. I would like to acknowledge in particular the encouragement given to me by Mrs. Doreen Grayson of Westport, Connecticut, Dr. Rodrigo Leal de Carvalho, Dr. Graciette Batalha, and Dr. Anabela Ritchie of the Instituto Portugues do Oriente; the advice and contribution given by Cecilia Jorge and Rogerio Beltrao Coelho, both well-known writers and researchers of Macao's past; the patience of my husband, who had to live through my many moods and a house submerged in paper; the enthusiasm and persistence of my daughters, who "pushed me out of the closet"; and last but not least, to my parents for having given me my story.

Prologue

1941, Macao, a Portuguese colony off the South China Coast

Yesterday

The wind is blowing strongly; leaves are everywhere, branches bent. The noise, that terrible noise stays inside me, although the tightly closed windows and shutters isolate us from the storm outside. I lean my forehead against the windowpanes, these unfamiliar stained-glass windows in this strange house! They brought me here tonight because it is stronger and safer against the force of the typhoon, and I try to look through the shutters into the night and the world outside.

The typhoon fascinates me! I am only five years old, but the tremendous show of nature in anger, this fury brought down on the city and the sea is something like a challenge to my imagination. It is the month of July, and the monsoon season has started.

The Pearl River on the far horizon is turning dark brown, with wisps of white foam. The whole island is rocked back and forth by the force of the winds and rains, and I think, *Will this force blow away the pains, the fears, the dark memories that lately have troubled my sleep? Will it blow away the old imposing house that I have just left for good, a few days ago, after death had paid another unwelcome visit? Will it crack its walls, bring down the roof, and transform this place into another ruin amongst so many others in this old city? . . .*

1

Today

My whole body pressed against the wide glass doors; outside the dark night was once again awakened by the force of the wind, the cracking of the rain! All of nature was again in a fury! And as I look once again, as so many times before, in fascination, into this uncertain, stormy night, this time through familiar windowpanes, in my own warm home, my own small family tucked safely away in sleep, I suddenly see reflected in the wet glass the face of a five-year-old girl staring back at me with the eyes of my past.

Surprised and frightened by this strange meeting of my childhood self, I ask her how she got there. Why did she come to meet me after all these years that separate us?

I begin to think about all the days, months, years that have passed between us. About all the roads, oceans, mountains I have crossed. The lives I have lived since then, to become what I am now. And, in awe, I ask her who gave me the wisdom and the strength to arrive at where I am today. Who led me up the road and where was she all this time?

Through the noise of the wind, the roar of the waves, the wetness of the rain, she answers: *Why so many questions? What is there to wonder? Just look around and see. The ruins are still standing, your roots are still deep in your birthland, no wind will be able to tear them away. Although everything changes, I am still you, your past, your memories, what makes you the person you are today. But if you want answers, look back, hold my hand, the hand of your five-year-old self, and let me help you to remember, remember . . .*

Chapter One
The Big House

Macao, 1941

Yesterday

I am in "Auntie" Molly's house, where my maternal grandparents brought me to spend a safe night. This house is bigger and stronger than theirs, and "Auntie" Molly is one of my grandmother's best friends.

It is morning. The weather is still grey and ugly, but the calm has come to the city, so punished during the night.

I am at the breakfast table next to my very young maternal grandmother, who is only forty-five years old. She is happy to be with her friend, and they excitedly gossip while I sit forlornly facing a hated plate of my daily porridge! But today it tastes different. My life is different altogether, and it frightens me. For a moment I lift up my eyes and see that those strange multicoloured glass windows are now open, and I let my very fertile five-year-old imagination wander out into what is going to be my today and my tomorrow. Windows fascinate me!

Where is that glorious window with brown wooden shutters up in the roof of the big old house where I used to perch myself, waiting for my seven-year-old brother to come home from school? It was the highest window in the whole house, and it looked straight down to the gates at the bottom of the three-level terraced gardens covered with beautiful Chinese porcelain vases with blooming roses. Lots and lots of stone steps to climb, where daily little and not so little feet would clamber, when all my cousins went out to play.

Oh yes! This house harbours old and young together. We are a big family, and it seems that tradition makes it a point that the sons in this family must make a home here. Uncles, aunts, cousins, my parents, my brothers, and myself, we all live on different levels and in separate quarters, but under the same roof, ruled, though quite silently, by the matriarch—my father's mother, a widow for many years.

This is my father's family house and we do not lack people in it! There are the happy ones, couples with children; the carefree bachelor who spends more time out than inside these walls; the spinster with a sort of question mark in her face, always awaiting orders from the old lady. Small orphans who seem to look at us with a lost look of wonder, we the privileged ones with loving parents. Many, many servants, some born in this family home, some as old as the stones that surround us, but all very faithful and terribly attached to this family and its offspring.

My father, out of his numerous brothers and sisters, appears to be the most successful and somehow stronger personality in his home. All my uncles and aunts have different personalities and lead different lives, depending on their own financial situation.

There seems to be very little happiness amongst the inhabitants of this house, and I can feel, already at my tender age, that lurking in the background, amongst all those many shadows, whispers, and secrets making their rounds, there is this lonely, unhappy woman, the spinster, an aunt, carrying her own heavy and dark secrets. I have overheard many times the servants gossiping about an impossible and forbidden love! She fascinates me and because she is my godmother, I pay more attention to her and can feel her sadness and her soul in turmoil. Her bitterness can be felt

4

in this house, which she dominates in the shadow of my grandmother, and her honey-coloured eyes become hard whenever she looks at the young brides of her brothers.

Somehow I am not happy here. I am shy, introverted, rather withdrawn emotionally. I often hear the family complaining that I am not fond of kisses and hugs. I can feel that the other children in this house, with their personalities, beauty, and energies, have sent me into the background, like a little mouse, as they call me, small, skinny, and sullen. I do not reach out and show my affection. Maybe without understanding the pain, I know it is there. I have already lost two baby brothers, and what my parents went through must have somehow gone into me. Also, there is war in the world, and on my island there are lots of new people who are called refugees.

I just want to sit at my windowsill and wait for my brother to come home from school . . . and there he is—jumping out of the car up the driveway, with his load of schoolbooks, looking up at me, waving and smiling with his mischievous and intelligent eyes!

I glow with pride! What I lack, he has. He is full of everything! He is the only brother left after the death of my two baby brothers, so I hold onto him. I cherish him. He is so bright and quick at everything. I have heard my parents say that in his class he gets ahead of the lessons by studying extra pages, and that the teacher had to prevent this by glueing the pages of the textbooks together. He is three years older than I, but he is not very big or tall; rather he is thin but full of bouncing energy, with a slightly Oriental look, especially in those slanted almond eyes that continuously hold a smile, a sunshine, a caress. He moves easily amongst all the cousins and mixes well with the grown-ups, while I hang tightly onto the hand of my *amah*, my Chinese maid. The white starched Chinese jacket and the wide cotton black pants seem to be a protective screen for all my fears and inhibitions. The only time I wish I could let go of her is when she does my pigtails in the morning. It hurts terribly because she braids them too tightly! But regardless of this pain, I do love the mornings.

In early morning all the window shutters open with loud banging noises, ours and those belonging to the other houses attached to us on each side—on the right the one belonging to my grandfather's older brother and his family and on the left the house belonging to my father's eldest married sister—making the three houses together a big compound, like a main house with two long arms stretched out, wanting to enclose something. Sometimes it seems like we all will never escape from here.

When the sun is up and there is a gentle sea breeze that brings to us the perfume of the roses in early mornings, happy sounds escape through all those windows.

Often two wives, the "outsiders," the ones who married into the family, sing songs each from their house, together making beautiful and cheerful duets from window to window, like a challenge to the forces of old traditions, and those are the moments I love best.

All these women look so beautiful! Some are young brides; some already have children. Some have definite traits of mixed Chinese-European blood, dressed always in the Chinese silk *cabayas*, the tubelike dresses with slits on the side. Some, not so Asian-looking, are dressed so elegantly with embroidered soft materials, fashionable Spanish mantillas fastened around their hips or lying over their shoulders. Their dresses reach down nearly to their ankles, making them seem so tall, standing so straight, like the lily flowers growing in the pond.

When their children are near them, there is so much warmth in their eyes and in their caresses, in every movement of their hands, as if suddenly by magic they are like animated fragile porcelain figures.

These are the women I admire in silence, trying to store in my mind all the details of their beauty so that one day I can be like one of them.

Soon this rare moment of music, serenity, and dream will be shattered by the rush of the morning duties: bed sheets are thrown

6

over the windowsills for the sun and the breeze to freshen, all those *amahs* belonging to different sets of families urging all the children to get started, some to school and some to play outside, the smell of breakfast with porridge, rice soup, coffee, little cakes, homemade butter, jams and marmalades from old family recipes, soft fresh white bread, a variety of tropical fruits, and hot, foamy fresh milk from the cows of the farm on the other side of the hill.

Then my mother would take me out by the hand to say good-bye to my father leaving for his office and to visit her favourite spot in the garden.

We go round the fruit trees, past the roses and the tropical plants, into where, under the shade of a huge rock where a thin stream of water trickles, lies the vegetable garden, with all kinds of Chinese greens, herbs, lettuces, tomatoes, and beans. Mother loves this place with its round stone table and benches. Now for a few moments she can forget the house and the gloom in it and I can silently admire her, my mother, so beautiful and such an "outsider"! A "caged bird" who came from different grounds and breeding. Her eyes are sad; too much suffering has come into her life too soon, too suddenly! She is so young, and yet she seems so wise and so poised. I wonder how her life was before, how she was when she was small like me.

I look around us and also wonder if these rocks, these walls, these trees have seen happier days when those who are old now were children, and how they had been. Had they been different from what we are now? Had there been a little mouse like me before? Had my father been like my brother? Had there been a beautiful doll with almond eyes like my favourite cousin? Had there been sadness or happiness in those days? . . .

Chapter Two
My Mother

Today

For questions asked there should be answers, and I cannot leave my reflection in the window wondering forever. I am a grown woman, and so many closed doors of my past have been opened since to my understanding. So the little five-year-old reflection of myself has to give way to the woman of today for this part of my recollection.

My mother was the oldest of five children born to a very unusual background. Her grandfather reached Macao as a young man, a bachelor working for the government, and he immediately searched for a bride in one of Macao's convents housing young orphaned girls. This was the usual procedure followed by most single men wanting to start a family. Soon he was married. His very young wife, having lived all her life inside the cloister's walls surrounded by nuns only, was frightened by the outside world and the responsibilities of a married life. Very soon after the wedding, she ran back to the convent. Forced by the nuns to fulfil her married obligations, she was never happy in her new life. She gave birth to one boy and two girls, and sometime after the birth of her third child she ran away from home, never to be seen again.

My mother's grandfather could not take care of his young children by himself but lacked the financial background to place them in good hands—the girls in the best convent and the boy in a seminary. The Church was of great importance to the society of Macao in its early days, and it was a privilege to be able to have destitute children well taken care of in good religious institutions.

The bishop of Macao had in high esteem this poor and desperate father, and through his influence my great-grandfather was allowed to place the two girls in the hands of the nuns of Saint Anthony Convent and the son was sent to the Jesuit Seminary of Saint Joseph. The rumour in town was that the young mother ran away with another man whom she really loved, but the children were told that she had died.

The two sisters grew up with only the idea of becoming nuns. Their education was centered towards this. They had no idea of what the outside world was like, thus not having the possibility of really knowing if this was their vocation. Strangely, their lives were patterned the same way as their mother's and in the same place.

The two sisters could not have been more different from each other: The one who was to become my mother's mother was beautiful, strong, rebellious, and outgoing. Her sister, although also beautiful, was shy, introverted, and very submissive. Their destiny was, of course, elsewhere. Luckily for them, there was a revolution in Portugal and the new authorities, not very sympathetic to the religious institutions, ordered all convents to close down. The two young girls were returned to their father, as well as the brother.

By this time my grandmother was fifteen years old. Her father immediately arranged for a marriage, and he chose a young man from the Portuguese colony in India named Goa, who had come to Macao to establish himself as an ophthalmologist. But one day her brother brought his best friend home to visit: a dashing young officer newly arrived from Portugal to join the army in Macao in the fight against the pirates plaguing the South China Sea and other areas. It was love at first sight for the very young girl and the twenty-year-old man. But they ran into stiff opposition from the angered father. The couple fought hard and, when forbidden to see each other, wrote passionate letters pledging to kill themselves if

9

they were not allowed to be together for the rest of their lives. Finally, after a long fight, the father relented and the young girl became a happy bride.

Once married she embarked with her husband into many adventures, leaving her city and her sheltered life to travel and live on unknown islands, into jungles and danger. She faced many lonely days without the protection of a husband, looking after her newborn baby. She was a young mother, at sixteen, with only the instructions left by her husband on how to use a gun in case she needed it.

When my mother was seven years old, her parents, a young sister, and two brothers were living on the island of Timor, in what was at that moment the Portuguese colony in Indonesia, an un-hospitably primitive tropical island. Her father was fighting in the jungles, and the young mother was bedridden, very ill with malaria. So my mother had to learn to take care of the household and her sister and brothers, the youngest being only a baby. It was a hard and hostile life for such a young child. It made a mark on her character and it strengthened her in her growing-up years.

Once my grandfather was transferred back to Macao, their life became more relaxed and easy. Soon another boy was born into the family. The children became, in their new and civilised surroundings, a handful, always active, sportive, a happy and mischievous bunch. Money did not flow in that family, and the children were taught to live very frugally and be content with whatever they had.

My mother, being the eldest, was the one to make more sacrifices for the benefit of the younger ones. But she was glad, because their love for each other and their closeness made up for all she didn't have.

Not belonging to the high society of the city, my mother's family did not have to pretend or compete with others and did not have to worry about criticism or gossips. They belonged to the middle class, so much richer in freedom. So my mother grew up with her love for sports and the outdoor life. She did not have to sit through stuffy society teas, fanning herself out of boredom, like other local girls her age had to do.

She rode bicycles down steep hills with both legs stretched out, not worrying about crashing and daring the boys to do the same. She was also a keen hockey player, and she boasted that her girls' team could beat the men's one at any time! With her brothers and sister and sometimes with her mother joining in, she would lead them all into all kinds of adventures, games, and lots of laughter. On some nights, she and her brothers would cover themselves with a white bed sheet and climb the walls of an abandoned cemetery next to their house to frighten the courting couples who sought privacy in the dark. But one night they met a couple who did not believe in ghosts and it was their turn to run . . . ! They were always full of mischief and fun, and soon they were joined by others who found their company very refreshing and their group became the liveliest one in town.

Although my grandfather, who was extremely strict in every sense, ruled his family with military discipline and more than once slid his belt off his pants for punishment, on the whole they were a very happy family and the house was full of laughter, with my grandmother often joining in the jokes and games; a mother who was more a friend and accomplice because of the small age difference between her and her children.

Surprisingly, my mother, with her beauty, was popular with girls her age, as she was with young men. She did not provoke jealousy because she was natural, unpretentious, and a great friend. Once, to help her history classmates pass a surprise exam, she sat in the front row, facing a very young, bashful male teacher, showing her legs under her skirt more than the teacher could afford to look at. So he turned his chair and faced the wall with his back to the whole class and to all the history books that suddenly appeared on the desks. The sad part of this anecdote is that this same teacher years later headed my history class, but by then he was older, wiser, much less bashful, and with an excellent memory! Like my mother,

11

I also sat in the front row, but for a different reason! My history classes were the hardest I can remember, with a teacher fearing repetition of an embarrassing moment like in the past.

Not all was fun and games for my mother. She also looked at life with a sense of responsibility, and when she finished her schooling she planned to go to Europe to enroll in a university. She wanted a higher education so as to become a professional. But Destiny wanted differently!

Chapter Three
My Father

My father was the fourth child of a family of twelve, born into centuries of traditions and roots on this island. His ancestors could be traced as far as 1660, when this island had already become a Portuguese colony.

Two hundred and forty years after, my grandfather and his elder brother built their houses on the slope of the highest hill on the island, facing the spot where the Pearl River languidly slid down over murky banks out of China, towards the South Sea, and where the first Portuguese navigators disembarked at the shores of the ancient Chinese temple called Ama-gao, from where probably the name of the island derived.

My ancestors formed their families and lived next to each other like feudal chieftains, carrying on the traditions inherited from the past, when a variety of nationalities enriched their blood. In its early years of existence, there were no Portuguese women in Macao and very few in Asia. The Chinese had forbidden their womenfolk to mix with the European men, so the Portuguese had to seek wives from various other places in Asia, where Christian women were available. Their sources for wives were Malacca (in Malaysia), where a large mixed-race Christian population existed; Japan, mainly in Nagasaki, where there was an important Portuguese community; Goa (India), and the Philippines. Also, many traders from Japan had installed their families in Macao. From these sources, the native-born Macanese originated. Much later, the

Chinese also intermarried. My father's family had all these roots, plus a Dutch grandmother.

Both brothers were well-to-do professionals, and their favorite pastime was collecting porcelain, antiques, and stamps. Gambling was also one of their weaknesses. In those days money was easily spent!

Wives were kept at home to have children and to care for their families and households. Not that they had heavy duties, for there were plenty of servants who grew up in the family through the years, passing from mother to child the same task and the same loyalty. Women were not supposed to be concerned with the men's business world or to worry about or question their financial situation.

In this circle of "natives," the ones with the longest-standing history on the island, there was an aura of laziness and passivity, especially amongst the older generation of women. Their favorite pastimes were going to church, playing mah-jongg with their beautiful and sometimes very valuable ivory and bamboo sets, cooking special food, and visiting friends.

The very rich array of recipes passed through the years, from generation to generation, a mixture of local, Asian, African, and European cuisines inherited from many travels of the navigators who through the years colonized the island, made the tables of these native households of the richest in variety and taste. The basic and most important food element was boiled rice, which was used daily, and around it on the table there were always other dishes, ranging from fish, chicken, and beef to vegetables, all with exotic and most unusual names. The kitchen was always the busiest place in a Macanese home!

Teatime was a special moment of the day for the ladies. There is no way one can describe the variety of cakes, sweets, and other delicacies offered. It was an exquisite time of abundance. If there was an occasion to celebrate, and this happened often, because people loved to entertain, teatime was the favourite meal, but it was a late tea, when the sun was on its way out towards the horizon, and

14

it was called Cha Gordo (fat tea), where not only sweets were served but also turkeys, roasted chickens, meatballs, and pies, a nonending gastronomic affair, accompanied by hot soups and special spiced teas from the Indies, jasmine tea from China, and, for the more conservative newcomers' taste, English tea. In summer, exotic fruit juices were added, the favourite one being fig leaves' syrup, a thick and aromatic delicacy.

Afternoons could also be spent at the Macao Club, a popular and traditional meeting place where one could sample the best Macanese cuisine and find a table to play cards. It was also at the Macao Club where all the special society events took place: wedding receptions, charity functions, cultural evenings, etc.

Women here also were very religious, and every morning and afternoon the churches would be filled with the old and the young, with their black lace veils and long rosaries. Churches were also meeting places where the old women of the island heard gossip from each other, chitchatting in the local dialect, and learnt news from the newcomers.

This island has secular churches in every main spot, in every square, up on the hills, in the centre of town. They are beautiful and grand, some built in the early days, and they all stand still against the wind and through the years have not become ruins. They are witnesses to the rich history of this island, registering the births, weddings, and deaths of all its inhabitants. Through the centuries an amazing collection of accounts of miracles, especially during combat times, when the island, in its beginnings, was attacked by the Dutch repeatedly, have been written in the archives of the island.

Women, because of their education in convents, were also very gifted with their hands, which from a very young age were taught not to be idle: knitting, lace making, embroidering, sketching, and piano playing were, amongst others, the favourite abilities parents wished to bestow on their daughters.

Men, having their womenfolk tucked safely and quietly at home, could indulge in a variety of games, entertainments, and travels and often had a minor wife and a second family. It was really a man's world, where he was the master and blindly obeyed and trusted by the rest of the family.

My grandfather was very well off and belonged to one of the founder families of this island. He was a well-known and respected lawyer. His life-style was grand, and he kept his family well provided with all the comforts and luxuries.

Not different from other men of his standard and wealth, he kept in a small apartment on top of his office a concubine, a minor wife, who bore him three children. She was Chinese and very devoted to him, not making any extravagant demands and accepting her background role. Her main task was to gather a small amount of stamps from his collection into little stacks, roll them into a tight roll, and bind it together with a fine thread which she would cut with the help of her front teeth. Later on, these would bear the mark of this delicate job; her front teeth showing fine cracks where the thread continuously cut through.

One day my grandfather's "sand castle" came tumbling down. An eager and regular attendant of the horse races that took place on the neighbouring British island of Hong Kong, he went there weekly. The stands of the Happy Valley racing course were made of bamboo and straw, and to feed the public attending these races makeshift kitchens were installed under the stands. At one of these race meetings, while my grandfather was chatting with two of his friends, one of them a Japanese businessman, and with Grandfather's minor wife quietly watching the scene, one of the kitchens exploded and soon all the stands were engulfed in flames and most of the people were trapped. My grandfather and his minor wife managed to escape, together with one of his friends from Macao. But the Japanese businessman was less lucky. Burning and in panic, he called for my grandfather to help, and despite the terrified efforts of his minor wife to prevent him from returning to the burning inferno, my grandfather went back to help his friend. Unfortunately, a burning beam fell on top of him and pinned him

16

down. His friend from Macao tried to lift it up, but it was too heavy and hot. So my grandfather became one of the many victims killed in that horrible fire. His half-burnt gold watch with his name engraved in its cover was found, to prove that he was indeed one of the unfortunate victims and also to enable the family to recover the charred remains.

My grandmother suddenly found herself in the midst of a great financial confusion, not having any knowledge of how she and the family stood financially and how much capital she had to survive with. The greatest asset my grandfather had, apart from the porcelain and antique collection shared with his brother, was a very important stamp collection, the profit from which would help her and the children to live comfortably. But this collection could not be found anywhere and there were no records or instructions left by my grandfather. Because women were kept in the dark about the financial side of life and did not share with their husbands or fathers the men's world of business, chaos broke out at my father's home. Gone were the carefree and lazy times!

Suddenly a saviour presented himself to my grandmother in the person of a rich Chinese man, owner of the most important empire of firecrackers. Many years before, this man, then a young boy, was working in an opium den and through his shrewdness learnt that he could make extra money by scraping the bottom of the opium bowls to retrieve whatever was left there and sell it. He was bright and hardworking, and soon his boss, recognizing in him a potential businessman, made him his partner. Through his early years as a struggling young man, he met my grandfather, who not only worried about his welfare but also gave him advice and became his friend, although so many frontiers separated them, socially, in life-styles and education. Through the years this man became a very rich and very wise person who knew the value of money by counting each cent he earned and saving the most he could, living as though he were not so well off, knowing that what he had earned was through hardship and struggles and not forgetting the helping hand he received from my grandfather when he needed it the most.

When tragedy struck the family, he remembered his debt of gratitude towards my grandfather and came forward to offer his generous help. He pledged to my grandmother a monthly sum of 300 patacas (Macao currency) to enable her to support the family until one of her sons could take on his shoulders the task of being in charge.

Although struck by this setback in their financial means, my father's family kept their life-style, their home, and their pride. Carrying on the traditions of great respect for the older generation, the widowed mother was accepted as the head of the family by her sons, although they were the men of the house.

Meanwhile, through difficult years of hardship, growing-up, and learning experience, my father, after working and saving enough money to support himself, managed to survive seven years of law school in Portugal and had the satisfaction of returning to his home and opening his own law office. Needless to say, the Chinese benefactor became Father's first client and stood by to see my father was making enough money to himself provide the 300 patacas to the family, before relinquishing his support. Throughout the future years until his death, he was my father's best adviser and friend. He was a great, wise man who did a lot for this island and its people, and as a homage to him, my father requested and got permission to name the street where his present home is built after his benefactor.

My father, together with his other brothers, who in spite of not having had the opportunity to travel to Europe had managed to get an education as well as form their own families, carried on the task of running the big household and supervising the education of the youngest member of the family, a brother who was born after my grandfather's death. The family traditions and life went on.

While finishing law school in Portugal, my father had heard of the unusual and lively girl, that bundle of energy and fun who was to become my mother, and on his return to Macao he wanted to meet her. From then on there was no escape for either of them. Their destiny was sealed.

The courtship was a turbulent one. My father, while madly in love, still found it amusing to flirt here and there, and my mother could not accept this situation. She made up her mind that she would be better off going to Portugal to further her education. She managed to get a scholarship and broke off with my father. On the day she was to leave Macao, there was a typhoon and all sea transportation to Hong Kong was stopped. Taking advantage of this God-sent respite, my father pleaded with my mother to stay and promised marriage and a life full of happiness. And so, abandoning her plans, she said yes to my father's request to share her life with him and left behind her dreams of independence, to become "an outsider," a "caged bird," her freedom gone, her laughs muffled, her tomboyish ways banned, in a household and in a family so opposite from her own. No wonder storms and typhoons have always attracted my attention and awed me. My being in this world is the result of one.

After her honeymoon trip to Japan, she returned to my father's house to find that most of her wedding gifts had been distributed amongst the women of her new home. These were the new customs she had to accept and follow. In her almost empty hands she held a small clay angel that had been part of the wedding cake decoration. To this day she cherishes this little, unpretentious reminder of her wedding day!

But love can do miracles and she did manage to bow to this kind of life and when her babies arrived, sons who were so important in that family's tradition, she felt rewarded for all her sacrifices. She had one son after another, and in that Asian society this was regarded as a great deed, because boys were the most important addition to a family with a name to carry to posterity.

Soon, though, even that was taken away from her! It was as if the house wanted to punish her some more, to make her more humble, to erase that beautiful and spontaneous smile she always carried! Out of four children she was left with two, and soon I was the only one alive, a girl! It was a high price to pay, and she started to feel the pressure and to resent the house and the family in it. She wished and prayed for a way out!

Chapter Four

After the Storm

Today

That five-year-old reflection of my childhood that I glimpsed on the wet window managed to penetrate herself deep in my mind and soul to become a second me and gives me no peace with her constant digging and searching of my past. She opened a door that is going to be difficult to close, because her five years will soon become six, seven, and so on. She'll grow through our recollections; she will go on telling her story; she needs to communicate, maybe because she had been such a silent child and now, strengthened and reassured by the woman she became, she can let go of all her restraints, her fears, her dark shadows, and release her past, to talk, talk, and talk. . . .

The physical years leave us forever and there is no way one can get them back, but the years of the soul, the sentimental moments of one's life, leave us only because we want them to, but never forever. They exist inside us, recorded with rings around one's heart like those in the trunk of an old tree, showing with every ring, and era, a step in our growing up. There is no way one can erase them, and I see now that it is so easy for our past to catch up with us and show us the power it has of sliding through one's mind, one's whole life, in only minutes.

This urge inside me to let go of one ring after another, releasing my heart through the silent voice of my five-year-old self, is

21

frightening, because it is like meeting myself for the first time! How many unknown memories hidden deep inside me will she bring out?

Until now my life was projected towards the future, never to the past. I have been married to an Argentine diplomat for over twenty-nine years and have three grown-up daughters. We have travelled and lived in so many countries, my children are now settled in different corners of the world, my married life has been so rich in experiences, so why are the memories of my childhood days invading me now, poking at my heart, making it hurt with the nostalgia for a place and a time so out of my reach? . . .

Macao, 1941

The wind and the rain have gone, and although everything is still wet and the streets are full of leaves and debris, we are returning to my maternal grandparents' home.

I remember now that the pain I carry inside me and hurts so much is the pain caused by coming down the main stairs in the old house, just a few days ago, amongst all those whispering people in the shadows, all in dark, dark rooms with shutters closed! *Why?* I asked myself! *When the sun is so bright and warm outside? Why all this gloom, this tragic atmosphere?*

Somebody was leading me out of the house as though he were "saving me from a fire" . . . ! Rushing and pulling against my short strides, which dragged because I was afraid of what was happening and what was going to happen.

I remember last night when my parents took me to that darkened room and to the bed at the foot of my beloved window, now shut tightly and so unwelcome, where that young boy with smiling eyes, whom I love so much, lay suffering, hardly breathing, and I was told to give him a kiss and say good-bye. Why? I was not going anywhere; I had my nightgown on, and I was going back to bed! So I kissed my brother and said only goodnight, and before leaving that dreaded darkness I looked up at the window, my window, and prayed for tomorrow to come quickly so that all this unhappiness I was touching would fly away once I was perched high on its sill!

I did not know then that my brother would never again look up at me and at my window; I did not know that this darkness was going to be his forever! I understand now that I will never again return to that room. The goodnight was, in fact, good-bye! The window never again opened its shutters for me, nor my brother his smiling eyes. I know that the dark shadows I touched that night will forever dwell somewhere deep in my heart.

I was taken away from the house so that I could survive. At least out of four children my parents could have one child alive. But I am a girl and the others were boys! Can I fill that empty space left by their deaths?

I realise now what illness means and what can be its outcome. To be ill for me meant being in bed, being spoiled and cared for, having lots of presents, people visiting, parents who sit next to you and hold your hand, and in the worst moments, when there is fever, pain, and suffering, there is always Mother's cool hand on one's forehead, Mother's kisses comforting you. I never minded being ill. I have been bedridden many times with what they call malaria, and so was my brother. Since the death of my two other brothers, my parents had been extra careful with us and most anxious about our health. Now I understand their worries, the extremes they went to, to prevent another death! Sending me to live separated from them, closing their ears to my cries of protest, is their utmost sacrifice to try to save me. There is something evil in that old house, something against smiles and happiness, and I must get away from it.

Now I am here at my maternal grandparents' small and modest house, in the same atmosphere my mother grew up in. It is very quiet without that army of uncles, aunts, cousins, and servants. Here I reign as an only child! Only three grown-ups live here: my grandparents and my mother's younger brother, still a teenager and

23

so good-looking. Now that I do not have those smiling eyes to look up at, now that my brother is gone, I find a substitute in my uncle, to hold onto and survive this loneliness. I am to stay here and never return to the old house to live. My father is quickly building a new home for only us three, and once it is ready we will again be a family, and in the meantime they are living in the Riviera Hotel, the best in town, and I must adjust to this sudden change in my life.

My parents come to visit me daily, with haunted looks in their eyes, so lost, my father leaning on my mother because she is the stronger one, she is the angry one! I wish I were grown-up so I could hold them both in my arms and ease their pain. I feel that my three brothers became me when my parents hug and look at me.

Each visit, my mother gives the same anxious instructions to my grandmother about what I can eat and what I can't, especially anything bought outside the house! About sitting away from drafts, not too many outings, strict hours in bed, washing my hands always, etc., and all the time my grandmother, still so young, looks at me with a twinkle in her eyes, and with a half-smile she winks reassuringly. I understand! I have already tasted this newfound feeling of freedom! Gone are the fears! I have had the fantastic experience of tasting all the delicious food the vendors on the streets have to offer, especially the crispy roasted duck and all the fried soya bean delicacies. My grandmother hates to cook and often resorts to whatever she can find outside her door, in the busy street. Oh! How we giggle and feel deliciously guilty when, having a mouthful of such food, we look at each other and remember my mother's severe instructions and what her reaction would have been had she walked in at that moment and seen us! My grandmother raised five healthy children in jungles and in houses much smaller and much more primitive than this one, and she fears nothing!

This house is made of laughter, of open shutters, of pure air and liberty! I come and go as I please! No more talking in whispers; there is a space for everyone, although military discipline still exists (I often look at my grandfather's belt with respect!); I finally feel like a person, no longer a grey mouse. My pigtails do not hurt anymore; I do not have a personal maid and have learnt to do them myself.

My grandmother keeps her energy running the whole day; she is so active, her long greyish-blond braids bouncing in the morning while she cleans and fixes her home. Mornings here are when the sun is hardly up. Timetables are respected by the minute. My grandfather leaves very early for his duties at the army head-quarters, dressed in his brown uniform with so many brass buttons! He is not tall or big, but to me he looks formidable. He is not communicative and most of the time he grunts instead of talks. I also think that he is a little afraid of me in his own way, afraid maybe of becoming soft on me. I know he loves me, maybe more than others in this house. I can feel it, but I will not let him know. There is not much show of affection; just a pat on the head will tell you he loves you. What a change from the strangling hugs and wet kisses I hated so much in the old house. This man who has fought pirates and who has freed the kidnapped children of rich Chinese families from their hands has lived a hard life! Because he seems so strong to me, I call him "Ahcong" ("Grandfather" in Chinese); it sounds more important to my ears.

Whenever my grandfather is not on duty and on the weekends, he goes to the islands that are also part of Macao and where he once fought the pirates. His favourite one is called Coloane, a huge mountainous island with beautiful bays and beaches of fine black sand. He walks up and down the hills with the help of his inseparable walking stick, which he uses to poke the bushes, unearth stones, and move small obstacles from his footpath. He has a sense of belonging on those islands, perhaps because it was partly due to him that the people, who are mostly farmers and fishermen, could now live there peacefully, away from the dangers of pirates.

He is friendly with everyone and is like a small king amongst them, although he hardly communicates with the villagers because of his Chinese—it's simply horrible! He and my grandmother speak a very funny Chinese due to their difficulty in mastering the many different tones in that language. He never learnt how to speak it properly, but nevertheless, they all understand him and he usually returned home from those trips loaded with vegetables, fruit, pigeons, and chickens that were given to him.

In the evenings after his trips to the islands, he would sit me on his lap and tell me stories of his past related to his days of fighting and his hopes for the future. He wants me to understand the importance of these islands, and he tells me that he is sure that there is gold on those remote, beautiful, and untouched mountaintops. I am always fascinated, listening to him. Those are the special moments when I feel less a child and get closer to this man.

He came from so far, from another civilisation, with another way of life, and still he gave so much of himself to these islands. He is a man of the earth; he respects every stone, every plant, everything nature has bestowed on us, and he is making me understand it. Our richness is whatever grows from under our feet. Nature will feed us, will help us breathe, will shade us, will surround us with beauty. Seeds for him are the greatest gifts. Whenever he has some in his pockets, he goes to the islands and, with the help of his cane, poking here and there, making little holes, throws them down, and in his future visits to those spots he takes so much pleasure in seeing seedlings grow. I am sure that half those islands' vegetation is the work of my grandfather.

Although with a rough character, a man of few words, he can be also a poet, when he talks about his islands. He is less communicative when telling me about his battles with the pirates. He is not very willing to go into details and tells me wars are cruel and a little girl like me should not be curious about fighting. But he does like to tell me how he saved so many children who were kidnapped by the pirates. Some were returned to their families, but others, too small and young to remember their names or where they lived, had to be taken to Macao and raised there, without their families.

The afternoons at my grandmother's house are usually very

quiet moments. After teatime, a very frugal one, she goes upstairs to a cool, big room to iron shirts, bed sheets, all the clothes we removed from the rope on the terrace a few moments before. They all smell of sunshine and the cool sea breeze.

I sit in a small wooden chair my uncle built for me, facing my grandmother, loving to look at her quiet, soft face with no wrinkles, so intent on her work, with the very heavy charcoal iron going back and forth. She sings or hums most of the time when she is doing this chore, but I put my two little hands to my ears: she does not have a musical ear and sings terribly off-tone! We always laugh and laugh. . . .

She often playfully gives me a newspaper and tells me to read the news, knowing that I can't read. I feel very important then. I cross my short legs, open the newspapers (usually upside down), and pretend to read her tales from my imagination. Daily I hear the grown-ups talk about the war and I don't understand anything of what they are saying. But to be part of their lives at that moment, hating to be left out, I look very intent and pretend I am interested. I can see they laugh at me and indulge me in my intrusion into their adult world. So when my grandmother irons, I read to her my own version of the war news: no more fighting, people all over the world are friends again.

I call my grandmother "Mama-Vo," a combination of Chinese "Mother" and a shortened version of Portuguese "Grandmother," and she loves it. Since I looked so grey, so unhappy, when I first arrived in her house, she took to calling me "Tadinha," short for "Coitadinha," the Portuguese words for "poor little thing"! We both are such great friends and have so much fun together. She taught me to fend off my fears, especially at night when it is dark and I am alone, telling me to say, every time we hear bad news or feel upset, "May the devil be deaf and dumb, blind, crippled . . . " and she would go on and on, adding all kinds of curses, and we all felt better. . . . !

There are many things I love to do in this house. I have learnt

27

to handle grown-ups, avoid their bad moods, take advantage of their best moments. Because I am the only child in this home I have to find a place that suits my playful mind and also the seriousness of those older than me. I try to fit in, and in this process I somehow have learnt to "blackmail" everyone into doing things for me. I know their weakness, and I use this knowledge. The "grey mouse" had lots of experience in studying people and personalities while living in the shadows of the old house! I also have noticed that the grown-ups also use me to get their way with one another. So we all play the same game! It is great fun!

I have also learnt in this house that one can handle bad moods by being cheerful. That's how my grandmother faces the dark moods of my grandfather. Whenever my parents had a fight, they would not speak to each other for many days. But whenever my grandfather picks a fight with my grandmother, he never reaches too far. My grandmother will just shrug her shoulders, look at my grandfather with a twinkle in her eyes, and say, "Me no worry, me no care, me go marry a millionaire! If he dies me no cry, me go marry another guy! . . . " and then will burst out laughing! She did tell me, though, that it is in a very bad English, but it is done on purpose, for rhyme and for fun.

Life here is not only centered amongst us four. There are visitors like my grandmother's sister, who also got married and has many children. They come very often to visit and it is always very lively and fun having them around. Also, we have neighbours with whom my grandparents socialize, although my grandfather is a very possessive and jealous person where it concerns my grandmother and does not encourage visitors. He cannot tolerate seeing other men looking at her. We have many times gone out for a walk and halfway through he would drag us all home because some man along the way had lifted his hat in greeting and stopped a little too long to stare at my grandmother! But how can they help it, she is so beautiful!

My uncle found a little playmate in me, a sort of pet. He tries so hard to please me, to entertain and amuse me, and I enjoy it. He never had, until now, experience in handling a small child. And I never had a grown-up giving me so much attention. I call him "A-tiu-chai," meaning "Small Uncle," half in Portuguese, half in Chinese.

He made a wicker chair on wheels, makes me sit on it, and with pride takes me out of the house for a ride. I really don't like riding on this chair because people on the streets stare at me curiously, wondering if I am a cripple. I want to shout back and say I am not and that I can walk and run. It's only because of the anxious instructions my mother had given that they treat me with extra care, because they are afraid that I'll fall ill again. I have never felt healthier!

In the mornings, my uncle wheels me on the chair through many streets with beautiful small houses, lined one after another, on to the Moorish Gardens (a name given to a small hill covered with all kinds of tropical trees and plants), which has on its top what the people of Macao call "Montanha Russa," the Russian Mountain, something like a twirling ice-cream cone made of cement where you go up and around and around until you feel dizzy. The going down is when I feel happy to be on the chair; it is then fun because we go crazily and dangerously fast! Going up makes my uncle very tired; he really has to push the chair with effort and sometimes has to stop midway.

Once up there, he sits down, opens a little basket, where hidden in a clean white cloth are two oranges, one for him and one for me, and peels them with a small knife. This small snack is like a banquet for both of us! We sit on top of the world, looking down at the busy city, its people, multicoloured, multinational, so picturesque! We talk about many things; my uncle tells me about all his dreams, of becoming a journalist, of going to battlefields and writing about all the soldiers fighting. He tells me he does not want to continue to study; instead he would like to go in search of adventure and to see other countries. I listen, fascinated, he has such imagination! He

29

tells me so many stories! We have lots of fun together, two people so different in every way, just learning to know each other.

Somehow I always find pleasure and happiness in high spots, looking down at people. First with my window in the old house, now here, on the Russian Mountain! I can hear the birds singing, smell the pine trees, feel the fresh breeze, and observe life going underneath my dangling feet. Colourful red and green rickshaws zigzagging by, vendors with their straw hats and heavy baskets at the end of bamboo sticks carried over their shoulders. I love to see them: the bamboo stick, so flexible yet so strong, giving rhythmic movements to the heavy baskets as if it were a slow dance. One can see more women carrying heavy loads than men, women dressed in dark, with black cloths hanging around their straw hats veiling their faces, protecting them from the sun. Children playing all kinds of games on the street pavements, housewives talking with each other through their house gates. It is a nice town; there are nice people; what an unusual leisurely life! I suddenly, for the first time, feel part of it all. No wonder I do not get ill anymore! There is so much life around me!

My parents often come to visit, and each time they do they are less tense. There are smiles on their faces, and they look down at me with less dark memories in their expressions. My reflection in their eyes shows a little girl who in these few months became less of a shadow. There is more light and life in here, and I think they feel more reassured.

I look forward to these visits, and I recognize the horn of my father's brand-new sport car, even when it is far away. They take me out with them for rides, and lately we go visit the site where they are building our new house. It seems so big!

I love the place; it is midway on the slope of a hill with a church on top. On the other side of this hill lies the big old house that I dislike so much! My father told me that he had bought all the land on this side of the hill. The new house faces the sea, and the view is just beautiful. The street is lined with huge old trees. I think I will be happy here! My parents tell me I will have a small playhouse just for myself in the garden, and I am thrilled and so excited! I can't wait for the day it will become reality and we three can be a family together again. I miss them both very much, but what I miss the most is sitting on my father's lap and feeling warm and loved. While others have always called me a little mouse and said I was ugly, he would call me his "princess" and say I was the most beautiful little girl! Now at night when I say my prayers before going to sleep, I add one more for the workers to quickly end the construction of what is going to become my new home.

Although I am happy with my grandparents' company, I feel the loneliness of not having playmates like I used to have amongst my cousins. I miss my parents; I miss mainly my brother; I miss the daily rituals, like when I went to bed and my parents came to say goodnight and I would say to my mother; "Boa noite Maezinha, querida, linda, amor," meaning "Good night, dearest, beautiful Mother, and my love," and also the same to my father. Even when they were angry at me . . . and I did not feel like saying it then! Also I miss having them call me "Didocas." Only they would call me this. Because my mother and I share the same name, there was a need to give me a nickname, which ended up being "Didi." I miss what my mother used to do whenever I had an eyelash fallen onto my cheek. She would gently pick it up, give it a kiss, and stash it inside her dress near her heart. She said this was for wishes to come true!

Many times I sit by the window of my small room, which does not have the view of my old high window. This one has a house in front of it, but with my imagination I erase it to see right through and look back to the memories I love.

Chapter Five
The Old House

The old house is perched on top of a steep and narrow lane made of cobblestones, which starts from a small square, shaded by a gigantic old tree, and winds up to stop at an elaborate huge iron gate. The narrow lane is called Beco do Lilau, the name, it seems, derived from the well in the middle of the square, where the residents get their fresh water. Every day there is a large gathering around the well, and often I come down to watch the Chinese women throwing a bucket attached to a strong rope down the hole. The rope just slides and slides, and the metal bucket makes all kinds of noises, banging on the sides of the well.

In the afternoons, I wait eagerly to see the crowd of visitors coming up the lane. Usually many young people from the neighbourhood and relatives come. These are the afternoon gatherings! My cousins range from small babies to teenagers, so the house is always full of different-size playmates. I seldom join the games, but watching them is already a great pleasure. They have slides, swings, wooden horses, little cars, bicycles, and a variety of mobile toys that take them from one end of the garden to the other. The three different-level terraces offer them a heaven of choices for privacy. The older ones separate from the younger, and many games go on at the same time. There are also some who mastered the difficult job of flying kites, and the different and exotic models are always a great attraction to the little ones to watch. The older girls gather somewhere else and play their own games, often musical ones. They sing songs and clap their hands and join together in circles. I have learnt all the songs, and at night, all by myself, I pretend I have my own friends and play their games, singing alone.

The adults in the main house and from the two adjoining ones would lean out on the windowsills to watch and, if the weather was nice and there was a cool breeze, often would come out and sit in the beautiful wicker chairs, sipping long, cool drinks or tea and following all the coming and goings of the younger generation with amused looks.

When it started to get dark, everybody dispersed into their own quarters and the whole area regained some of its tranquility. I sometimes believe that the roses seemed to breathe better after the rowdy group left and become more regal!

The hours in between, until dinner was ready, were the time when the adults played cards or mah-jongg or chitchatted, while the school-age kids did their homework and we, the smaller ones, searched to find a place to go in some corner of the house where we would not disturb them. In those hours, many of us were taken by the maids to the servants' quarters, where, taking advantage of the quiet moments, they would sit on low wooden benches drinking tea while all of us played together under their watchful eyes. They were not supposed to take us there, because each one of us had our own *amah* who took care of us in our own apartments, but I suppose they preferred being together so as to gossip rather than being separated and alone. Most of the times they had sweets or food bought from the street vendors and they would share that with us. I used to love the very sour and salty dried prunes, which made my mouth water and my cheek suck in! Also the sunflower seeds, mostly because I loved to lick the salt.

During those moments I opened more and more and became very communicative and curious. The maids spoiled me because I was the youngest of the girls and I was so quiet. So they told me stories, answered my questions, taught me their songs. I learnt many things about them: their customs, their past, their dreams. I know now why they all have different hairstyles: short straight hair, long tresses, neat buns, and even permed hair. It is their own way of showing whether they are single, married, or widowed.

The older maids, the ones with chignons, would go out once a week to *saw kai* (comb the bun), and several times I had the chance to accompany one of them down the slope of Lilau, to a nearby bench and table where an old woman would untangle the freshly washed long hair, which sometimes would reach lower than the waist, spread with the palm of the hand a greasy cream all over it, and comb it backwards, tightly into a beautiful and intricate twirl of knotted hair. I was fascinated to watch that gluelike liquid disappearing into the hair with the help of a very thin comb and then, when every strand was in place, the ceremony of cleaning the forehead of any unwanted hair so that the hairline was smooth and neat, holding the middle of a long thin thread with the mouth and with the two hands holding the extremities. With quick coordinated movements of mouth pulling and fingers sliding, the patterned thread would then pull even the tiniest hair out, leaving a smooth and beautifully shaped forehead. Usually all this was done once a week.

I also remember the moments when the maids had to prepare the almond or sesame tea: they would either let us hold the wooden handle on the very heavy stone grinder or let us pour water through the hole of the top stone while they ground the almonds or black seeds slowly, turning the two heavy stones carefully. It fascinated me to see the milky liquid squeezing out from between the stones and smell the aroma. I also used to love helping them wash the rice inside huge granite bowls with indentations on the inside much like veins on a peeled orange; I was hypnotized by the hands passing once, twice, so many times the rice round and round on the inside of the bowl with water washing away all the starch until the grains looked transparent! These movements of the grinder and the hands washing the rice will, I am sure, be always remembered by me.

In the evenings, when the sun was starting to hide behind the hill, was the time I started to shrink within myself. The house became darker; all the shutters were shut closed. All the dark antique furniture, the porcelain statues, big mirrors, and grandfather clocks, made strange shadows on the walls; the long wooden floor boards cracked with each person passing; the glass chandeliers, which at one time in the past were used for candles, hung heavily from the ceiling. So many rooms to cross, so many dark halls, so many naughty cousins, aware of my nonexistent courage, coming out to frighten me . . . !

All this darkness and frightening shadows would become light and fairy-tale moments when the old house woke up to get ready for a special occasion, a party, a celebration. Especially if it was for Christmas!

Oh! How I loved Christmas! When I remembered the parties I felt a little pain in my heart, a little sadness for having missed the Christmas party at the big house this one year. In my Mama-Vo's home we had a very simple one, so different from the ones in the past.

Partial view of Macao, taken from Guia Hill in 1933

Partial view of the old "Big House." My parents' apartment and my "window" appear in the middle of the top story.

Married sons and daughters surround the matriarch of the Jorge family, 1935. My father and mother appear on the far left.

My mom, my eldest brother, Adolfo, Jr., with the "smiling eyes," and myself, *center*.

The Machado-Roque family. *Front row:* my mother's brothers, Tomas and Pedro. *Back row:* my maternal grandmother, my grandfather, my mother's cousin Hilda, my mother's aunt Julia, my mother's cousin Branca, my mother's younger sister Maria, and my mother, circa 1930.

My parents' wedding—September 3, 1933

A happy grandmother surrounded by some of her grandchildren in 1936 (she had thirty-five grandchildren altogether).

My mother and aunt Phyllis—the "outsiders" and "caged birds"

Mother and the "Little Mouse," dressed up for carnival time

My father with the Chinese benefactor of the family, Hon. Kou Ho

The new house on Penha Hill (below the Penha Church)

The new, tiny member of the family (with me), bringing so much joy
six years after the tears.

Chapter Six

Christmas and New Year and Other Festive Occasions

In the big house, each married couple had a huge Christmas tree in their quarters and in the main hallway there was a gigantic one decorated with heirloom crystal balls, gold and silver ribbons, an assortment of decorations passed on from generation to generation, lovingly cared for, wrapped in silk cloth and kept in special places, to be opened with great expectations in front of the younger generation, so eager to participate in the excitement of discovering each piece and hanging it on the tree.

Very early in December, the decoration of the house started. All the vases in the garden were planted with Christmas season flowers, windows were washed and decorated, floors scrubbed and waxed, and there was an air of excitement in every room.

Sweets were made especially for the occasion. The Macanese have a very rich array of traditional food. At Christmas many sweets had a meaning for the celebration, like the "mattress of the Child Jesus"; the "pillow," which was my favourite, made with cornstarch dough and a coconut filling; the "windmills," twirls of thin pastry covered with candied sugar that the Macanese said were the "blankets" of Jesus. I used to sit for hours in the kitchen, fascinated by the way these windmills were made: by just twisting a stick in the middle of a flat, thin, square dough, inside a pan filled with hot oil. In every household of the island this sweet is a must. Once cooked, it was kept in a special container made of glass, extremely large in size, with a silver cover. I loved to stare at these containers in anticipation of what I would find inside them at Christmas and also because they were as big as me!

In our quarters my mother used to outdo herself in the most beautiful decorations. She used red velvet ribbons, the longest strings of silver and gold pearls, beautiful coloured wrapping papers, and our tree was a sight to remember. I have seen many pictures of my baby brothers under the same tree I shared with my big brother, but I do not remember any Christmas with them. I was too young when they died.

The night before Christmas was full of excitement. The kitchen was full of action preparing the food for the supper after the Midnight Mass. Only the very young ones would go to sleep early and not be able to share that part of the festivities. I was still too small and never joined the grown-ups after they returned from church. But before going to bed I went and spent some time gazing at the enormous table covered with the most exquisite handmade lace tablecloth, the beautiful old Chinese blue and white dishes, silver trays, and all the food. Sometimes, if I woke up in the middle of the night because of the noise downstairs, I could smell the aroma of the freshly made hot chocolate creeping up into my room, the way it is done in Macao, with a very well beaten egg yolk with lots of sugar, the best cocoa powder, and boiling hot water! There are special large, round cups for chocolate, and when it is done this way, it fills to the rim with the most delicious brown foam! I could never go back to sleep then. I would lie awake, anxious to have my brother come into my room to lead me to where the tree was, and while waiting for our parents to wake up from their late night, my brother and I, we stared at all those packages; we touched them with the tips of our fingers to try to find out their shape and what they might have inside. My brother would then tell me everything about the night before and share with me his excitement. I did not believe in Santa Claus anymore, because I had too many grown-up cousins, and listening to them I came to the conclusion that it was my parents who put the presents under the tree. I even had the courage to sneak sometimes behind my mother's back to see what she was wrapping.

Then when my parents finally woke up, we had a wonderful time exchanging gifts. Usually mine were the best. My parents really spoiled me! Then we would put on our best clothes and go down to join the rest of the family and receive more gifts.

For lunch we sat around the big table, which had been emptied of all the food and decorations from the night before and rearranged and redecorated for this meal. It was great fun to stare at all the candies, nuts, and crackers that promised small treats inside! The food was very special for this occasion and very traditional. I disliked the first course, which the grown-ups fussed so much about: a broth of fine rice noodles with small shrimps, and we had to add from a side dish thinly sliced pickled carrots and turnips, which were prepared long before Christmas. That soup had a sour taste that I just could not find easy enough to swallow! Ah! But the desserts! That would make up for all the other strange food.

Right after lunch, the table was cleared to make place for another tablecloth and another display of food, this time an assortment of cakes and pastries for the visitors. Relatives and friends would come by during the afternoon, a long procession of people coming and going, everyone coming with a gift and leaving with another!

In the afternoon each couple and their children would leave the big house and do their own rounds of visits, the first one being to the two houses next to ours, visiting my father's eldest sister and my father's uncle's family. It was the time of the year that my shyness would disappear and I was most willing to accompany my parents everywhere and would give my kisses freely to anyone! I was getting so many packages in return. At the end of the Christmas season, my brother and I had tons of presents and our parents would select some to give to the less fortunate children, the poor ones whose Christmas days were not as blessed as ours.

The bad thing about all these visits at Christmas was that once you visited someone, in return the person would have to repay you the visit before five days, so for days and days all the grown-ups were busy going somewhere or having visitors at home. By the time it seemed it was going to quiet down, then you were facing the New Year festivities.

My parents always said that I spoiled one of their best planned New Year's parties. They were going with a group of friends to Hong Kong, by ship, but I was born at two in the morning of the thirty-first and the party was called off! Having a birthday on such a date was no fun for me because people were always thinking of the New Year's Eve party and rushing for the preparations. Plus on the last day of the year there was in the afternoon the Te Deum at the cathedral. People of Macao are very religious and nobody misses this church service, which is to give thanks for the year that is ending.

I did have a nice birthday party, and my mother always baked the most beautiful cake with candles and lots of delicious food, but somehow I always felt that there was a kind of rush. Anyway, I enjoyed it: the noise, the excitement of seeing the grown-ups getting dressed up, the men in elegant tuxedos, the women with beautiful long dresses, the dinner preparations, and the decorations for the occasion. All this gave me the chance to take part in two worlds: that of my age group at my birthday party and the other glittering and sophisticated adult one.

For the New Year, the smaller children were allowed to stay up. Anyway, who could sleep when the longest string of red, angry-looking firecrackers would be lighted up at midnight, turning the whole neighborhood into an inferno of noise, enveloping the house in clouds of smoke with a terrible acrid smell! The *amahs* told me that this was a tradition and it was to frighten the evil spirits away and to clear the air around the house for the New Year to enter it with everything that was good. If our parents were home, then we had a party together and at midnight everybody jumped on top of a chair, a sofa, a bench, anything that was high, and on the last stroke

47

of twelve, everybody had to jump down with the right foot touching the floor first, for good luck.

The next day, family, friends, and government officials received and returned courtesy visits, and these again, as on Christmas, before five days passed.

The Chinese New Year came a little late, sometimes at the end of January or in February, depending on the new moon. The big house had very little time to quiet down and find its normal rhythm after the last festivities before being hit again by an effervescent rushing about with preparations for this occasion. Although it was not something that the Macanese celebrate, the close relationship that everyone had with the Chinese community made it a must to share in it. It was also so much fun to watch everybody working.

All the women of the household joined together their efforts in making, with their own hands, beautiful cherry blossom flowers out of paper that would adorn huge towers of wooden trays holding each other up with pillars, all wrapped in pink or red silk paper, with layers and layers of sweets and candies. These trays were given to all the rich and important Chinese friends of the family or business acquaintances. It was a tradition, and it could not be missed. Also many cakes were made and then wrapped in red cellophane paper. For the Chinese, red is very important to bring good luck.

The first day of the Chinese New Year, which runs for three days, my brother and I were dressed in red Chinese silk clothes, with little red Chinese brocade hats and red silk shoes. Because it was always the coldest time of the year, the clothing was lined with wool and we looked so fat! The best part was when we got to visit my parents' Chinese friends. Once we bowed to them with hands joined together and wished them Happy New Year in Chinese, we were given small red envelopes with gold lettering. Inside there was money, and sometimes, depending on the importance of the family, it could be quite a sum. Our parents usually took it and emptied it into our piggy bank. Because my brother was older than I, he sometimes kept some small amount to buy whatever he felt like.

This was not only a tradition of the rich. Even the servants followed this custom, but only the married ones. The single girls were not obliged to do it. The *amahs* gave us, first thing in the morning, their red packets with only new, shining golden coins inside, for good luck. We, the small ones, must wish them a good year before getting the envelopes, and we all learnt a very "greedy" way of greeting them! All of us in chorus would chant, "Kung hei fat choy, lae see yap toi," which means, in rhyme, "We wish you good luck, but put the red packet in our pocket"! The *amahs* would giggle and pretend to be shocked by our "greediness" and shower us with coins.

Again this very special time of the year would bring us special food, this time from old Chinese recipes. In every Chinese household, on beautiful rosewood tables, there would be a display of little dishes with lots of candied fruits, nuts, and seeds, especially the very hard red watermelon seeds. There was also so much noise, because everywhere people played mah-jongg, banging the little blocks against each other when they shuffled them on top of the tables, which sometimes were made of marble, and also because firecrackers were thrown here and there nonstop! On that day nobody could dust or sweep the floors because it would be like chasing the good fortune away. So the cleaning of the house was done the day before.

The main attraction of the festivities was the "dragon dance." There were many dragons, small, big, dancing in the streets, accompanied by drums and firecrackers. These dragons, led by a funny Chinese clown, fed themselves with money notes hung on the windows of all the houses. It was a custom to attract the dragon to your window so that after "eating" your offering, he would then perform a colourful dance to bring you good fortune for the rest of the year. When I was small, I used to be afraid of the long wiggling beast, but then later I noticed that the multicolour scales were made of silk and were carried by legs belonging to dancing men, hidden under the layers of cloth.

Again, for this occasion, the garden of the old house had to be decorated, and the vases that had held the Christmas flowers now had beautiful little trees with lots and lots of miniature tangerines on them. Some other bigger vases had cherry and peach blossoms. In the whole house, there were dishes spread everywhere, each with watermelon seeds, make-believe gold coins, usually made of chocolate, and a small tangerine in it. In all the Chinese homes, at their doorstep small tables were set with food and lighted incense sticks as offerings to the spirits. I heard the maids say that the New Year time was hard on their pockets, although every working person got double pay. But all the debts had to be settled before the New Year began, and also every family member must have a complete new set of clothing and new shoes.

The first months of the year seemed to be full of activities. Soon after the Chinese New Year, we approached the Carnival time. Another busy time! Again all the households were buzzing with excitement with preparations for the three-day event; everybody had to have at least two sets of costumes. There were grand parties at night with masqued balls. For the children there were also many parties, where prizes were given for the best costumes. As usual, my mother excelled in making those. My brother enjoyed being dressed up, but it was a dreaded moment for me. I shrank even farther away; always standing behind him and feeling utterly ridiculous all dressed up, looking like something out of my storybooks. The Carnival parties ran for three days, and every single one of them had at least two parties going on. They were held at different places, for the children in the afternoon and for the adults in the evening. The main one always was at the Macao Club. At those parties I just couldn't find the courage to mix with other children—the noise, the games, and the confetti flying all over our heads, that rain of multicoloured squares of papers that suddenly covered our hair and even got into our mouths! I was not a participant but a watcher, and it was difficult to make people understand my way of being. So on those occasions I became like an unapproachable "house pet" (a *bicho*, like they called me in Portuguese) and my mouth began to have a turned-down look or puckered lips as if I was about to cry.

But when it was the turn of my parents to participate in those parties, I enjoyed it! I always looked forward to watching my mother preparing her costumes and dressing up in so many extravagant ways. She had such imagination! And she always looked so beautiful. My father resisted being turned into anything else but himself. He never wore a costume but was always enthusiastic about my mother's. He looked almost amused at her innovations and was so proud of her successes.

How wonderful to be able to sit and daydream about all the past's good moments! But then, I also felt a sort of pain inside me, and I really did not know if I preferred the life I had before, so rich in so many things but so dark in so many others, or this one I had now, although I knew it would be only temporary. This one was so simple, so uncomplicated and undemanding: the days followed each other without surprises or unexpected things. Maybe I should concentrate on the days that would come in the future when I would live with my parents again in our new home.

But my mind cannot stop thinking, cannot stop remembering! There is a sort of hunger in me to bring back all the days that I know will never return to me again, to try to store forever in my mind my whole life with its richness in quality that only now I can appreciate, now that I have lost it. I feel I should be blamed for not having enjoyed it fully like the other children.

So I still need to dream and remember. . . .

Chapter Seven
Remembrance

My parents had lots of friends in Macao who did not belong to my father's family circle. They were all from Portugal, the expatriates with no roots in Macao. I heard the Chinese call them *guai lo* (a sort of "foreign devil") or *gnau sok* (cow's odour)! They were government people, doctors, businessmen, and other professionals, all very outgoing, sports-oriented, and extremely elegant. They were free to do what they wanted and not, like most Macanese, bound to the island's traditions and rules.

With a group of his friends introducing him to hunting, my father developed a great love for this sport. He would go away for days, either by boat onto the river to hunt wild ducks or by land into China and its mountains to shoot partridges and other game. It was always exciting to see him return from these trips with so many ducks or other birds and join the maids to pluck the feathers and look for bullets.

Sundays were family days; every member of the family as well as friends came over for lunch or tea. I enjoyed the cakes and all the special sweets that were served then. As we had such a large extended family, there was always a birthday to celebrate, but when there was no special reason forcing us to spend Sunday at home, there were countless exciting places where our parents would take us.

Some sunny afternoons we would have picnics on the grassy shores of the freshwater reservoir, a huge artificial lake overlooking the Pearl River. There the gentle breeze would play games with the silvery clear water and my eyes followed the beautiful patterns made by the soft waves, utterly fascinated.

From the top of the banks of this reservoir, one could look down over the small airport of the city. Many private planes were parked on its narrow, short airstrip, and on some sunny afternoons we would see them flying, light planes playing games in the air, thrilling us with their acrobatics.

On summer Sundays, we used to go to the waterfront in front of the reservoir and the small airport, where there were many bamboo and straw huts built on stilts over the seawater; there the grown-ups and the children who knew how to swim would jump into the water. I never could understand why they found it so exciting; the water was usually dark brown and looked dirty to me. In the same area was the small beach of Areia Preta (Black Sand), the narrow strip of land linking us to China. Seated on the coarse sand, we could see the ancient and majestic arch the Portuguese built a long time ago to mark our border.

Also we would go around the island in my father's car, slowly enjoying the views, waving at friends along the way, stopping at many fishing huts, which abounded along the bay. I was always fascinated by the huge nets that when in the water could not be seen, but that the fisherman would slowly raise when approached by an interested fish buyer. What a fantastic sight, the dripping wet net coming out of the water bearing small and big fish jumping desperately up and down with the sun shining on their wet skins, making patterns like dancing silver stars. My father, who was a keen fisherman in his spare time, enjoyed picking the best fish out of the nets, scooping them up with a long bamboo pole with a basket on one end. For this he would have to walk out from the hut onto a very narrow bamboo bridge over the water up to where the big net was.

Many mornings, some mothers with younger children not yet school-age, including myself, would get together and take us to Guia Hill, a beautiful place covered with rich vegetation and crowned by the oldest lighthouse in Asia. There were endless resting places with round stone tables and benches, miradors where one could sit and look into the horizon at the two other islands that also are part of Macao: Coloane and Taipa.

These outings at Guia were my favourites. There was so much space around us, so many shaded areas under the trees, that I could always find a little corner to be by myself. I usually sat on some narrow stone steps and in an empty cigarette can I would make a concoction of sand and leaves, turning it around and around with a short twig, letting my mind wander, watching other kids play, or further away into the soul of my island, admiring all the lordly homes around this hill. This was a privileged zone, and all around it there were beautiful old houses and palaces where the descendents of this island's founders lived. Each of these homes was like a page of this town's history.

They were built in the colonial style—lots of terraces, verandahs with white columns; porches with elegant rattan furniture and huge fans on the ceilings; plants and Chinese porcelain vases with many varieties of flowers. Every house was built to give an impression of it being cool and shaded, because this is a tropical climate (although we also have winters), and the outside would be painted in pastel colors like pink, green, blue, and brick, its borders and decorations always in white. They often reminded me of cakes elaborately decorated with white icing.

For eyes that were not trained to notice any other particularity in a house other than the different style and shape, a very important detail would go unnoticed. There was in most of them something that an old traditional Chinese science influenced, a small change, an addition, an extra something. It was called "Feng Shui" (The Wind and the Water, which reigns over the destiny of a person or a place). Depending entirely on this, a house could be a lucky or unlucky place for its owner. It was very important for a person building or buying a property to consult the Feng Shui specialist. Depending on the orientation of the house, how the bad winds would blow into it, how the evil spirits could be attracted or avoided, extra windows would be added or removed, roof corners redesigned, an extra wing added, the main entrance reoriented, etc. Also, when the house was finished lucky charms would be placed in strategic sites and corners, like chimes, hanging mirrors, porcelain figures, mostly of the Chinese lion, and incense burners, gold and red papers glued to the walls, etc. Without a good Feng Shui, shops could go bankrupt and homes could harbour diseases and unhappiness.

For the less sophisticated Chinese family, a very simple and easy method was employed: A small child, a toddler, would be taken into the premises. If this child started to run all over the place, it meant that there was good Feng Shui. If, on the contrary, the child held onto the hand of the person who took him or her in and started to pull towards the door like he or she wished to leave, then the Feng Shui was bad.

Having big houses and plenty of servants, people in Macao were very fond of entertaining, making the town a very lively one and a favourite spot for visitors from Hong Kong. There were always tennis, hockey, and regatta championships between the two islands, followed in the evening with very grand dinner-dances.

Not all the festivities were frivolous ones. As this was a very religious place, all the Church celebrations were highly observed with pomp. Services in churches, processions, etc., were attended by everyone in Macao.

Chapter Eight
The New Home

Today

It is now time to stop for a while and let the layers of memories, which have been going on from the small child emerging from the past to the grown person I have become today, settle themselves in their own dimensions.

The reflection I glimpsed on the wet window has now become such a strong and permanent presence inside my mind that our voices get entangled: one that brings back bits and pieces of past memories based mostly on emotions and impressions that left a mark on the child and one that receives them and tries to fill in the gaps and analyse the situations. It is so difficult to distinguish the two!

What I see as the voice goes on is a child who felt lonely, although surrounded by so much love, wealth, and care. But I have also learnt, through that voice, that a lonely child, a forlorn one, is not really always a sad one. On the contrary! There is so much more insight, so much more maturity and wisdom, so much more sensibility kept deep inside that silence and withdrawal.

I also am glad that I saw in my reflection a grey mouse, such a shadow in the middle of so much light and activity. She was able to observe and store in her a tremendous amount of memories and treasures of my past. She is allowing me to record a time of life, a style of living, of a place that will never come again.

The mixture of two civilisations, two cultures, in surroundings so unique in such a special time, had tremendous influence and put a permanent mark on any child born on this island. My five-year-old reflection was not an exception to the rule, and so many things that I, in my growing years, did not know how to explain, things happening in my inner self, in my reactions, now fall into place, have their meaning, and I am learning a lesson of life.

The somewhat tragic voice, which for moments brought back so much pain and also laughter, has quieted down slowly. The little girl is leaving me, fading into her own dimension, her mission accomplished. I will be forever grateful to her sudden presence in my life, for the gift she has given me of my past.

But not all has been told. She is only five years old. What about her growing-up years? She will become six, seven and grow older. What of the days that belong to those years? How can I summon those voices? They are the future, still unknown to her!

There are so many memories of the past that are important, moments that fill in the empty spaces of our puzzle. For the sake of my little companion, to make her presence grow on, I will have to reach inside this tunnel of my past for her other voices, her grow-ing-up ones.

We will have to switch sides at the windows. She will be the listener and I the storyteller. These new voices will be less lively, less vibrant, then hers. The little girl is growing up, and with the years passing, she has learnt to accept situations and live with her present. The voices talking to me are sporadic ones, coming out only from some incidents and moments that must have marked my past. They only tell me parts of that growing-up childhood. But I will accept this, at the same time missing more and more that beautiful and warm flow of memories that came to me through that poignant little voice, my companion for such a long time!

Yesterday

After so many years of marriage, this is the first time my parents have a place of their own, alone, living undisturbed, walking freely in their own territory. I can see that they are happy finally. They have survived the grief, the mourning, and woken up to a new beginning. My mother has the home she always wanted and fought for for so long. Now she and my father can start life anew, like turning the page of a book.

They have set a new pace in their life-style. They are surrounded by the energetic and outgoing expatriates from Portugal, whom the war made temporarily "overstay" their term of duty in this colony. They are a close-knit group who prefer sports and doing fun things to playing cards indoors. Before their movements were restricted, they used to go around always innovating new adventures. One of their favorite pastimes was going up the river in a comfortable motorboat, deep into the mouth of the Pearl River, and sightseeing along its banks, admiring the pagodas along the way. I cannot but remember their physical appearance: the ladies with wide-rimmed hats and light-coloured dresses, looking so cool and fresh, the men with shirts and khaki pants and straw hats, all seated in comfortable wicker chairs on the covered deck of the boat, sipping cool drinks.

These special moments will never return to us again, and I feel so glad I was able to have taken part in them. My parents and their friends also met very often at the tennis club by the waterfront. It was a meeting place for the whole family: those who did not play would just sit and watch the games; some ladies would knit or embroider; the children played in the background surrounded by their *amahs*. This group of expatriates belonged to the strong, socially placed people, some working in the government, some doctors, teachers, businessmen, etc. They all had children older than I, but I didn't mind because the children accepted me amongst them and shared many of their games with me. Amongst this group there was the family of our doctor. The eldest daughter, a teenager, spent a lot of time in our house, and she and my mother got along very well. Influenced by this reminder of her younger years, my mother was full of mischief when with this girl. They played merciless tricks on my father and also on me. I remember one night, while I was washing my teeth in my bathroom, I was terribly frightened by two black-faced persons with turbans on their heads. They looked like characters out of my storybooks. They left me shaking with fear and laughed all the way down the corridor.

All this excitement, this new change of life-style, in a new house, was not easy for a small child to assimilate. When the simple and easy routine of my grandparents' home was just making its mark on me and I was feeling completely at ease in those surroundings, I was, once again, taken away to start another kind of life.

Although I was very happy to be able to be with my parents again, I felt the weight of the big new house, and reigning in it as an only child catapulted me to an unknown dimension.

When I think back to the first moment I entered this house, knowing it was for good, that this was our permanent home, lots of mixed feelings surged into me.

I remember the cautious first steps when my father led me up the long marble stairs leading from the street up to our gardens. I remember the awe and the funny mixture of excitement and regret that gripped my heart.

Led by my father's hand, I went through cool verandahs, spacious rooms, up a long curved staircase into a huge lighted hallway and what was going to be my living quarters: three big rooms and a bathroom. All that for myself alone! The house was being built when my brother died, so part of all this is his. I felt a little afraid and lonely, having so much space for myself. But when I saw the huge collection of dolls filling the glass cabinet that covered a whole wall of my bedroom, I thought all was a dream.

The room was beautifully decorated in pink and white, with some baby blue here and there. My bed, in the centre of the room, even had two steps to climb up it. Over the bed a huge mosquito net hung from the ceiling. There were large shutterless windows everywhere, facing the beautiful bay and the sea. It was difficult for a small child who went through so many changes in a such short while to grasp the real meaning of this new experience: finally a home, a real home!

What my father built was very grand. The house was enormous: shaped in a horseshoe. In one side there were two floors and on another four floors; the outside was in red and white, and spacious gardens surrounded it. I even had a small play-house with two rooms for myself in the garden. Next to our house my father also bought a big piece of land that he converted into a farm, with pigs, rabbits, turkeys, all kinds of vegetables, fruit trees that were planted by my Ahcong! Part of it is a slum area where some poor families live. All this land and the house are on the hillside opposite where the old house is. The hill is a very important landmark of Macao, because it is crowned by a very beautiful church where the bishop of Macao has his quarters. It is called Penha Hill. Now it has become a sort of Jorge Hill, because the family is spread around it. My father showed me that he bought all the land up to the top of the hill, and it would be great fun to be able to climb up to the Penha church from my garden. The view from the church grounds is breathtaking, overlooking the entire town, all the water around, and the other islands surrounding us.

The house had twenty-five rooms and lots of hallways and terraces, and to take care of all that, we had many, many servants. They had their own quarters and garden, which I specially loved. There were orange and lemon trees planted there amongst round marble tables and benches and beautiful porcelain and earthenware barrels that collected the rainwater. In summer the servants ate outside at round tables, and I sat nearby enjoying their chit chatting and the beautiful aroma of boiled rice, which they cooked in special clay containers. It was so much fun to watch them eat with their chopsticks dipping into the small dishes with salted fish, salted eggs, Chinese sausages, and other delicious and very aromatic foods.

How I enjoyed the space around me! No more grown-ups peeking out of the windows, no more cousins rushing around! All was mine; I was free to come and go, do as I like. The "grey mouse" became a sort of "rabbit," running here and there continuously discovering places, corners, and exciting views.

The silent child also found out that she could have a playmate within herself, someone out of her fantasy, and so started a new way of life, without loneliness, without hiding places. It was the crowd and the noise that made the child revert into herself. The life as an only child, the lack of other children around her, made her find the strength and the self-confidence she so much needed.

Living amongst grown-ups, listening to them, being accepted by them, made me more mature, opening up without restraint. Gone was the shadow to give place to the light!

I had a companion, a young lady who lived with my parents. She was an older version of the "grey mouse." She was orphaned at a very young age and thought she could find a safe life in a convent being a nun, but unfortunately her health was not strong to withstand the hardships of a convent life, so my mother took her in. She found a home with us and sewed for my mother. She was an artist with her hands. She embroidered beautifully and made rag dolls with huge blue eyes and long blonde tresses. She had infinite patience with me, and she gave me a sense of security, peace, like a corner where I could go and hide myself. She did not make demands on me; she accepted and understood what I was. Her name was Celeste, but because it was difficult for me to say it, I called her "Cessie."

Cessie was my storyteller. She knew so many fairy tales, so many legends and real-life stories! She never got tired. At bedtime I asked her again and again to tell me the same story. She learnt most of them at the convent and from reading so many books. I suddenly had a tremendous thirst for learning. My mind was ready to record all the beautiful words I listened to, to transform them into my own fantasy, and my loneliness was crowded by thousands of characters manipulated by my newly discovered silent dreamworld. Cessie also taught me religion and prayers. Now I looked at the churches of this town with a kind of awe, because I understood why they were there. The night prayers kept me safe from bad dreams, and I felt protected.

It was a lovely time! My parents were happy. My father was a very powerful and successful man on this island, my mother a very popular and beautiful young woman, so vivacious socially. They were the ideal couple, very sought after for parties and outings. It was a time for laughter and to start a new life.

Little by little I had lost the looks and the feelings of a grey mouse and was enjoying this new experience of coming out of the shadows.

The people who knew and frequented my parents' home were from all walks of life of this town: from the governor and his family to the simplest man on the street. My father had the door of our house open to everyone. He had not forgotten that once he needed help and was given a hand. So we had with us those who came for fun, for parties, for friendship, those who came for business, for advice, and for help.

The house was always crowded with visitors, but some were more special than others, like my father's family benefactor, who continued his relationship with us and very often came and visited, sometimes alone, sometimes with his wife. Through the years he stayed very traditionally Chinese and led a frugal life, although he was one of the richest and most influential men on this island. My mother always cooked his favourite food, and he enjoyed eating at our place very much. He was very much part of this family, and my father respected and admired him highly. He always had time to talk to me and would often hand me a red packet with money inside.

Another special person who was a regular visitor was my father's best friend, a very tall and big man with his head always shaven. A twist of destiny made him one of the Chinese children who were kidnapped by the pirates and later saved by my grandfather. He made my Sundays a very special day.

Sunday mornings I woke up to a very familiar and comforting sound, something that made me jump up from my bed very quickly. Somebody was in the garden pruning the roses, and it went "clic-clac, clic-clac"! It was not an automatic sound, but one that had an irregular rhythm, because the hands that were holding the scissors were caring and loving hands, doing a chore that had become a ritual performed every Sunday. Those hands belonged to this huge man. He came early, while everyone was asleep, waited patiently in the garden, and then joined us for our Sunday breakfast: the steaming bowl of rice soup with lotus seeds, fish balls, and long fried sticks of dough that were dipped into the soup.

I was often with him in the garden and loved his company. He had a special nickname for me: "Chupeta" (a baby's pacifier), because he said I had not gotten rid of my puckered lips, my sucking mouth! He teased, challenged, and consoled me. He was married to a very nice and warm Chinese lady, and they had many children. Sometimes they also came on Sundays, and I always enjoyed their company.

Would my grandfather have dreamt that one day the little boy he saved could become such an important part of our family's life and such a good friend of this little "mouse"?

The friends who came to visit my parents all had children older than I. So I had to learn to play new games, to "grow" a few years ahead of time. Because I felt a certain difficulty in mixing amongst the girls, I joined the group of boys, becoming a sort of "mascot" for them. They did not send me away but accepted my presence and enjoyed taunting me to do impossible things. I started to grow into a tomboy! I rode bicycles all around the grounds of the house, fell down so many times that my knees were always bruised and the wounds left ugly scars. Although I was suffering from malaria, there were days where I was bouncing with energy and looked forward to the most daring games.

One afternoon some of the grown-up boys had a bicycle race in my garden and I was taken by one of them as a "passenger" on the backseat. Unfortunately, our ride ended rather drastically with me falling flat on my face with my lips cut open on the stones of the garden grounds.

As there was no tetanus vaccine left on the island because it was wartime, the only way to prevent an infection from that wound, was to burn the broken skin off. So every night our family doctor would come and I would be seated on a chair in my bathroom, with my mother holding my head and my father my hands. Then the doctor lit the fire of a small alcohol burner and heated the blade of a knife, which was then applied on my bruised lips, with this process removing the damaged skin. It was like the fire was on my mouth; the pain was excruciating! But I had understood that it was the only way to prevent and heal any infection. For six nights I had to endure this torture. At the end my lips were a mass of deformed flesh. I remember one night when my parents stopped by my bed and, thinking I was asleep my mother bent over my mosquito net, looked at me, and sighed, saying that as I was a girl it was a pity that I was going to have deformed lips. The same will that had made me survive the illnesses surged forward in me, upon realising what my mother meant! I promised myself that my lips would be healed and that I would not look deformed.

This new life I was living was made of a mixture of happiness and pain. It was wartime and the days were filled with tragedies and people thought only of survival, of hope. It was a time for growing up fast.

Chapter Nine
The War Years

The war continued and it was time for worries. We had too many refugees, too little of everything else. Chinese, Europeans (mostly White Russians from Shanghai, French, Germans from all over China), Hong Kong residents, all the people who managed to escape the onslaught of the Japanese in the area, crowded our island. It was a big problem for such a small town to tackle. All the hotels and clubs and most of the private residences shared living quarters with refugees. There was lack of space, of food, and of medicine. But the Macanese never lacked the warmth and generosity that for centuries inhabited their homes: it was a time when people got together and tacitly they formed like a big family group, where there was no lack of helping hands and sharing was a top priority. The will to survive, to go on with life, was stronger than fear, the anguish, and the hunger.

At home there was always food, due to my mother's ingenious cooking and the insight of my grandfather, who planted all over the grounds, in spite of my father's continuous protests, banana and papaya trees, vegetables, and other seeds he brought from the islands. The experience he had acquired with the years living in the jungle, where one could survive with little variety of food, helped us to avoid starvation. My mother, with her stamina and perseverance, used to travel from one point of the island to the other to find fresh meat, so precious for our diet, sometimes in the very early hours of the morning or in the middle of the night. Some Chinese would brave the dangers of being discovered by the

Japanese and swim the narrow river channel separating us from China, bringing with them water buffalo.

It was also the time for me to learn about pain. I was again ill with malaria, which I had had when smaller, and each time it was more difficult to fight it. My small body tried in vain to absorb all the shaking and the high fever. The nausea was the worst part. I pitied my parents, who in the moment of crisis, when I was shaking so hard and feeling so cold, tried everything they could to save my body from the violence of the seizure. They covered me with so many blankets; they hugged me with their bodies. I could feel in them the fear of another death, the desperation of being unable to stop my suffering. They spent long nights of vigil, without any sleep; they bribed, cajoled, and fought their way for a little more quinine, so difficult to find. Some very dedicated friends and even strangers with big hearts sometimes could smuggle bits and pieces from Hong Kong whenever the Japanese were not looking.

Because the quinine was not having the required effect on my malaria, the doctors tried anything on me just so I could survive the war. Some treatments were painful and very expensive.

It was time for tears, for suffering, for punishments, endearments, and even violence, because facing my stubbornness in spitting out the very expensive and bitter quinine pill, my mother one day nearly broke my arm to try to force me to swallow it. I just couldn't! It was far too bitter, and my stomach really felt bad afterwards. When I was not ill, everything was easily forgotten and life looked so bright and happy. Unfortunately, malaria lingered on. I never managed to attend school regularly and had to study sometimes at home with a private tutor.

Doctors in Macao had their hands full with so many people ill, suffering, and dying from various diseases and epidemics. Many also died from hunger, sometimes in the streets, and most of the men refugees had to work as special police to reinforce the local contingent, to act immediately and bury the dead, to prevent the danger from those who were desperately hungry and went looking for food at any cost!

The refugees were given shark meat to eat, and many developed skin problems due to the toxin in that meat and their fingers were covered with blisters. These could only be healed by applying olive oil over them, in the absence of other medication. My mother, when the war was declared, rushed to the markets to stock up food and felt an urge to buy a huge quantity of olive oil. Thus many refugees, especially those at the Bela Vista Hotel, next to our house, benefitted from her large store of provisions, which she very gladly shared with them.

My mother took extra care with me, as so many children were ill on this overcrowded island, and she isolated me from most of them. Only children who were healthy and came from clean households could play with me. One of my cousins told me that her mother scrubbed and inspected her all over before she was allowed to visit our house. The fear was so deep in my parents! I was the only survivor of their four children; they had to keep me, against all odds.

I knew that most of the children envied my life in the sense that I had so many material things. I knew also that they whispered amongst them that I was a princess, and many did not want to befriend me. Even in wartime, my parents managed to give me the best clothes, the best shoes, and all the toys they could find. I was a "princess" in their eyes! Little did they know how I wished to change places with the other children, run barefoot, eat whatever I felt like, have freedom, and be a nobody, instead of being in the spotlight all the time and watched over so closely!

I wanted to tell my parents that I was tough, that I could fight this illness, that I could manage to stay alive, if only I could run, play, and eat like other kids. But how could they know this, if I had in the past been such a silent kid, such a "grey mouse," looking so weak and sad? But I did have my sunny days in my grandmother's house, my Mama-Vo's warm home where I was a "nobody," where I was treated as normally as possible.

If I was called a princess, then this title was valid in the sense of the love my parents lavished on me. I knew of their sacrifices, of their sleepless nights, of their caresses, of their soft eyes looking at me protectively.

We prayed for the end of the war to come quick and tried to carry on life as best we could. People pooled together their various abilities and talents, and we were blessed with numerous concerts of classical music, singing, and dancing. Orchestras were formed and every night was a party night. We also had excellent seamstresses, and old clothes became new ones with different styles. Artists immortalized the beautiful and exotic sights of the island. There were so many ingenious people who were willing to share, with those who wanted to learn, their knowledge. So it was a time of strong human relationships, of dedication, companionship, and unselfishness, and a time for miracles.

Every day was a new day, when pleasures and happiness were found in simple things. Somehow people managed to laugh, to have fun, although surrounded by tragedies. We were reminded of the war around us when, at night, we could see on the horizon the glares of the bombs falling on Hong Kong. Those who managed to escape from there during that time arrived exhausted, physically and mentally hurt by their ordeal, and told us horror tales.

My parents told me that we were not at war, that Portugal was neutral. We were spared the fighting and the soldiers, but the fears, the sufferings, and the hunger existed around us. Somehow some of the Japanese army was also on our island, but they did not bother us and carried on with their business and life quite isolated. The family of our doctor lived next door to the Japanese military headquarters. The two boys and two girls had a game going on: every day they would silently creep up to a window of their neighbours' house and manage to look inside. They said the Japanese had a very big map on the wall and they pinned little flags all over it. The amount and the places of the Japanese flags changed often, and they would report it to their father, who by studying a map could learn where the Japanese were advancing or retreating. Soon there were very few flags and we guessed the war was ending.

Chapter Ten
The Sunshine Days

Macao, February 1947

My forehead is, once again, pressed against the window of my room. Outside the sun is bright and shining. There are no clouds, no wind, no storms or dark shadows!

In front of my eyes lies one of the most beautiful scenes of this island: graceful, majestic Chinese junks slide through the brownish waters of the river, carried away by the soft breeze, with their large sails of hues of brown, humming and dancing against the blue sky. There are big and small sampans, as they are called. They are going out towards the open sea to start their daily routine of fishing. On the sides, their huge and black nets, already out on the water, trail a silvery line over the waves. Because it is so quiet, I can hear the voices of the fishermen shouting from one boat to another. This is a scene I have so often admired through these years living in the new house. I make a point to be at my window in the morning and at dusk, when they all come back and everything turns to gold: the dying sun with its last rays illuminating the half-closed sails. These are moments to daydream!

It is Sunday and my big shaven-headed friend is here. But this time he is not pruning the roses. The house is unusually quiet. There is a sense of expectation, of tense excitement, in the air. Inside this house something big is going to happen, something that means new hope, new happiness, a new beginning!

As I pause in front of my window and feel that the day has

suddenly stopped and we are suspended in time, I see, rolling in front of my eyes, the last events of this year of freedom, this year without fighting, without war.

So many things have happened to my young life! With the end of the war came the evacuation. A ship arrived to take away the sick and those who wanted to return to Portugal.

My parents had to sell the beautiful house to raise the money to take me on that trip, and bought a tiny one-bedroom house in the same area, not on our beloved hill, but facing it. We stayed there for a short time before embarking on our three months' journey to Lisbon. We went to all the major Portuguese ports in India and Africa and kept on taking more and more people on board. It was a long trip in a crowded ship.

Once in Lisbon I was placed in the hands of a very skilled and kind doctor, and soon my father had to leave us to return to Macao and his work.

So it was a time for separation, a time for mother and daughter to know each other better. It was a lovely time! All our old friends in Portugal tried their best to make us feel at home and less lonely. We lived in a hotel very comfortably, and I was terribly spoiled by its staff. My health improved and so did my personality. I think my mother had great fun discovering me, and we were good company to each other.

Because it was such a bright time, because the shadows had left us for good, the future looked like a big Christmas tree, and the best gift of all was placed under it: the promise of another child in our family! So, when the time came, we had to rush back to Macao so that it could be born there.

My mother and I embarked into a new adventure, our first air travel, by a sea-plane, which took six days to bring us back to where we belonged, to the arms of my father and again to our big house, which he had managed to buy back.

So I am once more daydreaming! Once more looking out of a window! This same rite so many times repeated through my life, but today I seem to notice that the sky is bluer and clearer than other days. It must be a good omen.

The birds are singing; the waves of the sea calmly break against the rocks of the bay, making a regular soft sound, so soothing and musical, coming to my ears like a lullaby, and enveloped by all this harmony, I lift my eyes up to the blue, clear sky and ask God to bestow on my parents His divine gift of a son, to make up for the three they had lost!

Suddenly a strange sound, one I've never heard before in this house, breaks this whole peaceful scene: the first cry of a baby just born into this life!

My father bursts into my room and with tears in his eyes hugs me and says, "We have a boy!" At that moment his whole body was like a giant of strength, of joy, of pride, and as I hug him I feel the vibrations of a new flood of blood in him, the blood of a new will to live, fully and happily, a man finally contented! And I felt, for just a tiny short moment, a sadness, a lone tear dropping down my cheek, a sort of regret that my hugs and my kisses were not needed anymore to erase those past haunted looks of sorrow he sometimes had when he thought of his sons.

But soon my own heart was filled with joy! The young girl at the window had lots of space available in her heart: she would keep forever her beloved brother with smiling eyes, safely and warmly in a special corner, and had already opened a big space for the tiny new member of the family who was bringing so much joy, six years after the tears.

Before the laughter, the joy, the happiness could settle permanently in this home, there is necessary still another intervention from the old benefactor of the family. Just as in the beginning of my father's life, now again he came into our house with a last gesture of help, of assistance, to the son of his old friend, this family whom he protected so jealously all his life.

He had seen the suffering my parents went through when they lost their three sons, and with his wise Chinese knowledge of old beliefs, of things that one cannot explain but do exist, of omens, of superstitions, of magical rituals, of good and bad luck, which befall one without any logical reason, he came forward and told my father that he was certain that my parents were not lucky with sons and that the only way to prevent another tragedy was for him and his wife to adopt symbolically this little baby boy immediately, so as to absorb and erase that bad luck themselves.

And so, following an ancient Chinese ritual, my new little brother was wrapped in a very old ceremonial red silk cloth and placed in the arms of the Chinese lady. I noticed how my mother cringed with fear when she saw how old and dusty-looking that cloth was! Then the old man placed on the head of the baby a red silk cap with gold coins hanging all around it. Both man and wife said a few words, a sort of prayer accepting the baby as their own, and immediately after gave him back to my mother's waiting arms. The evil spirits could not, from now on, disturb the happiness that was reigning in this household.

So the circle closes! Something once taken away is given back! I know that from now on the smiles and the happiness of my parents will be wider and fuller.

Today

. . . and with this new beginning I shall stop my book here, unfinished . . . ! Because there cannot be an end when death has been put far behind and the future is made of light, hope, and *life!*

While there is memory, while there is love for a past that makes our future, the ruins will survive many more storms and will stand forever against the wind.